LEWIS CAPALDI

DIVINELY UNINSPIRED TO A HELLISH EXTENT

ISBN: 978-1-5400-6127-0

Visit Hal Leonard Online at
www.halleonard.com

Contact us:
Hal Leonard
7777 West Bluemound Road
Milwaukee, WI 53213
Email: info@halleonard.com

In Europe, contact:
Hal Leonard Europe Limited
42 Wigmore Street
Marylebone, London, W1U 2RY
Email: info@halleonardeurope.com

In Australia, contact:
Hal Leonard Australia Pty. Ltd.
4 Lentara Court
Cheltenham, Victoria, 3192 Australia
Email: info@halleonard.com.au

GRACE

WORDS AND MUSIC BY LEWIS CAPALDI, EDWARD HOLLOWAY AND NICHOLAS ATKINSON

'Til I found sal - va - tion in the form of your

your grace, _____ your grace, _____ your grace, _____

___ don't take it a - way. _____ Your grace, _____ your grace, _____

___ your grace, _____ don't take it a - way.

BRUISES

WORDS AND MUSIC BY LEWIS CAPALDI AND ROBERT EARP

hope that you'll come back when you can find some peace,

'cause ev-'ry word that I've heard spo-ken since you left feels like a hol-low street.

I've been told, I've been told to get you off my mind

but I hope I nev-er lose the brui-ses that you left be-hind. Oh, my Lord, oh, my

ooh). _____ (Ooh, ooh, ooh, ooh, ooh, ooh). _____

It's your love I'm lost in, your love I'm lost in. Your love I'm lost in and I'm

tired of be-ing so ex-haust-ed. Your love I'm lost in, _____ your love I'm lost in. _____

Your love I'm lost in, _____ e-ven though I'm noth-ing to you now.

HOLD ME WHILE YOU WAIT

WORDS AND MUSIC BY LEWIS CAPALDI, JAMIE HARTMAN AND JAMIE COMMONS

Recorded a semitone lower.

on - ly I could wake you up, _____ my love, my love, my love, my love. __

wish you'd told me this be - fore, _____ my love, my love, my love, my love. __

Won't you stay a while?

Won't you (Hold me while you stay a while? _____

Stay a while. _____ Stay a while, _____

my love, my love, my love. __ Won't you stay a while?

SOMEONE YOU LOVED

WORDS AND MUSIC BY LEWIS CAPALDI, BENJAMIN KOHN, PETER KELLEHER, THOMAS BARNES AND SAMUEL ROMAN

Moderate Ballad

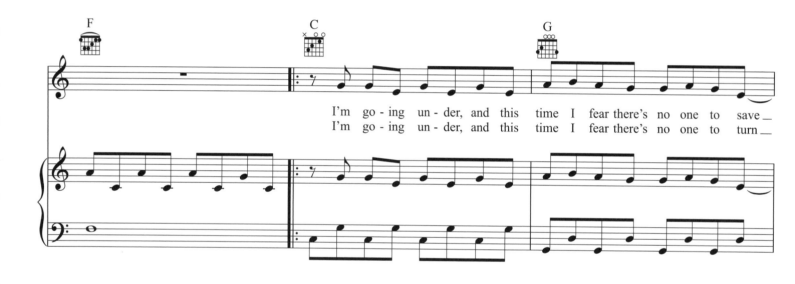

I'm go-ing un-der, and this time I fear there's no one to save __ me.
I'm go-ing un-der, and this time I fear there's no one to turn __ to.

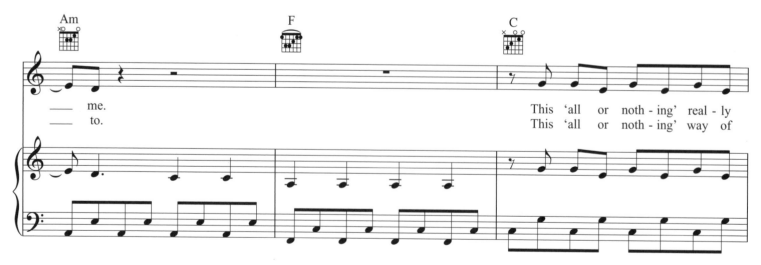

This 'all or noth-ing' real-ly
This 'all or noth-ing' way of

Recorded a semitone higher.

MAYBE

WORDS AND MUSIC BY LEWIS CAPALDI, EDWARD HOLLOWAY AND NICHOLAS ATKINSON

FOREVER

WORDS AND MUSIC BY LEWIS CAPALDI, SEAN DOUGLAS AND JOSEPH JANIAK

*Recorded a semitone higher

lie,   re - mem - ber.   No - bo - dy said that it would last   for - ev - er. ____

For-ev - er. ____   For-ev - er. ____

For - ev - er. _____

No - bo - dy said that it would last   for - ev - er.   That does - n't mean we did - n't

ONE

WORDS AND MUSIC BY LEWIS CAPALDI, TOMAS MANN AND PHIL COOK

DON'T GET ME WRONG

WORDS AND MUSIC BY LEWIS CAPALDI AND JAMIE ALEXANDER HARTMAN

47

49

when you come too close. _____ Don't get me

wrong, _____ I'd love to stay too _____ long. _ Don't get me wrong, _

I'd love to tell you what-ev-er you want _____ but have-n't you had e-nough of

lone-li-ness? Have-n't we had e-nough of sec-ond best? Don't get me wrong.

HOLLYWOOD

WORDS AND MUSIC BY LEWIS CAPALDI, KANE JOHN PARFITT, PHILIP PLESTED AND JOHN STEWART

Moderately fast

Out of fo - cus, did - n't take a sec - ond to no -

- tice. Now ___ we're sep - ar - a - ted by o - ceans vast. ___

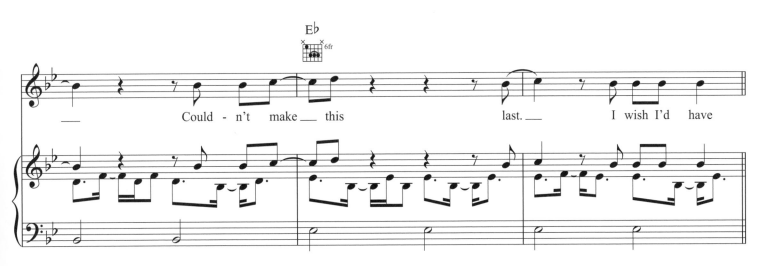

___ Could - n't make ___ this last. ___ I wish I'd have

CODA
Eb   Bb

back to the start? Oh, and you   know I would   if I could.   May-be I spend more time in

Eb   Gm

Hol-ly-wood   than I should.   So tell me, hon-ey, oh, when___ you're just a step a-way from

F   Eb

fall-in' a-part,___   do___ you ev-er feel like go-ing back to the start?

Bb   Bb/D   Eb

If you can hear me, does it real-ly have to end?   I feel you

LOST ON YOU

WORDS AND MUSIC BY LEWIS CAPALDI, DAVID SNEDDON AND ANUROOP PILLAI

Ev-'ry day ___ I'm a slave ___ to the heart-ache and you're

wast - ing a - way ___ ev-'ry night, Don't ___ wan-na leave you lone - ly, but I've

run ___ out of love this time. ___ You know that I a - dore ___ you, though I

could - n't give e - nough, ___ hope you'll be

FADE

WORDS AND MUSIC BY LEWIS CAPALDI AND JAMES HO

to tell the truth, I can't be-lieve we got ___ this far. ___

Run-ning near on emp - ty, _____ I wish some-bo-dy would -'ve told me ___

that I'd end up so caught up in need of your de -

- mons. That I'd be lost with - out you lead-ing me as - tray, ___ guess that I'm a

65

HEADSPACE

WORDS AND MUSIC BY LEWIS CAPALDI

ALSO AVAILABLE ONLINE AND FROM ALL GOOD MUSIC SHOPS...

ORDER No. AM1009712

ORDER No. HL00233553

ORDER No. HL00295684

ORDER No. HL00292769

ORDER No. HL00250373

ORDER No. HL00262694

ORDER No. HL00283140

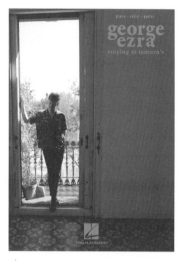

ORDER No. HL00283917

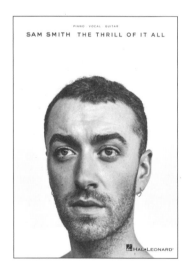

ORDER No. HL00257746

ORDER No. AM1013661

ORDER No. HL00243903

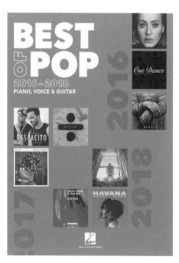

ORDER No. HL00283138

Just visit your local music shop and ask to see our huge range of music in print.

www.halleonard.com